CW01657966

HOW TO TYPESET YOUR PROJECT REPORT

IN

LATEX

A Ready Reckoner.

Mr Aniruddha S Rumale.
Mrs Abhidnya A Rumale .

IASER
Only Truth Matters
Indian Academy of Scientific & Engineering Reaserch

HOW TO TYPESET YOUR PROJECT REPORT IN $\LaTeX$

A Ready Reckoner.

by
Mr Aniruddha S Rumale
Mrs Abhidnya A Rumale

First Edition: March/April 2013

ISBN:978-93-5104-926-5

Published by
Indian Academy of Scientific & Engineering Research(IASER),
an Online Open Access & On Demand Publication house,
Flat 01, Anuj Apartment, Amarsimha Colony,Malegaon-Bk,
Baramati, Dist-Pune, Maharahtra , State-413115, INDIA
`http://iaser.in`

Indian Price: INR 150 ~~(without DVD) INR 200 (with DVD)~~
International Price: ~~US $ 15 (without DVD)~~

Acknowledgement

To prepare this small manuscript of our first edition we almost spent a half year. We know that there might be many things left untouched by us in this book; but, it contains all necessary instructions, ready to use templates, and basic information of LaTeX.
At present more than 2500 researchers and programmers are contributing to the development of LaTeX. And with this book, we are just trying to spread their work. There are many people who helped us directly or indirectly, and We are very thankful to everyone who helped us in this work.

This work is dedicated to our parents, teachers, and to the originators of LaTeX

Mr Aniruddha S Rumale
Mrs Abhidnya A Rumale

Preface

This book is useful for people in engineering and education for writing project reports, seminars, conference / research papers. LaTeX is becoming more popular day by day due to its excellent typesetting and ease of use. But there is no good book available in market which can talk in terms of the need of student and / or researchers. This book is a ready reckoner for typesetting a good report/book using LaTeX. It covers all necessary and essential information of LaTeX required to typeset a good report/book.
While typesetting our reports/books , we found that, out of 2600 packages, we hardly used not more than 20 packages. And, if the report/book is heavy in text then many time not more than 5 packages are ever required to typeset it. This showed us a definite structure to follow for typesetting a report/book.
Though this book is written for windows users, users of other operating systems can also find it useful as LaTeX and TeXMaker (a cross platform LaTeX editor preferred by us to write and compile the .tex and else files of LaTeX) are platform independent.
Contents of the books : Brief introduction to LaTeX Installation , essential LaTeX commands and document structure with step by step explanation of how to typeset a project report in LaTeXṪhe companion CD/DVD contains all chapter-wise source codes, all essential tools for LaTeX installation on Windows , and ready templates to create your report/book.

Mr Aniruddha S Rumale.
Mrs Abhidnya A Rumale .

Contents

Acknowledgement **i**

Preface **iii**

1 Installation **1**

1.1 What is LaTeX ? 1
1.2 Essential and supportive softwares 2
1.2.1 How to install the softwares ? 3
1.2.2 Installing Ghostscript 3
1.2.3 Installing GhostView 3
1.2.4 Installing MikTeX 4
1.2.4.1 Configuration of MiKTeX 4
1.3 LaTeX using command line 5
1.4 LaTeX using TeXMaker 6

2 Enter the LaTeX **11**

2.1 History of LaTeX 11
2.2 LaTeX versus WYSIWYG word processors. 12
2.3 The basic LaTeX File structure. 13
2.4 LaTeX commands and special characters. 15
2.5 Errors in LaTeX 17
2.6 Files in LaTeX 17
2.7 LaTeX packages 18
2.7.1 The Preamble of report/Book 21

3 LaTeX Commands & Environments 25
3.1 Text-mode commands in LaTeX 26
3.1.1 Text style & size manipulation commands . . . 26
3.1.2 Text handling in LaTeX 26
3.1.3 Accents & Special Characters/Symbols 28
3.1.4 Selecting Fonts for typesetting 29
3.1.5 Labelling & cross-referencing 29
3.1.6 chapter, section and part 31
3.1.6.1 Styling chapter names 31
3.1.7 Boxed text 31
3.1.8 Colored text 33
3.2 Math-mode commands in LaTeX 33
3.2.1 array and equation environment 34
3.2.2 eqnarray environment 36
3.3 Environments in LaTeX 37
3.3.1 Creating tables 38
3.3.1.1 tabular environment 38
3.3.1.2 table environment 42
3.3.1.3 table spanning more than one page . . 42
3.3.2 Importing Graphics 45
3.3.2.1 Creating graphic using Dia 46
3.3.2.2 How to include graphics? 46
3.3.2.3 figure environment 49
3.3.2.4 Text wrapping around graphic 50
3.3.2.5 subfloat command 51
3.3.3 Creating lists 52
3.3.3.1 Unnumbered lists 52
3.3.3.2 Numbered/Ordered lists 54
3.3.3.3 Descriptive lists 55
3.3.3.4 Inline lists 56
3.3.4 Theorems,Lemmas, and proofs 57
3.3.4.1 Theorem styles 58
3.3.4.2 Changing Theorem Numbers 58
3.3.5 Footnote, marginnote, endnote 59
3.4 Bibliographies in LaTeX 60
3.4.1 thebibliography environment 60
3.4.2 Using Bibliographic database(s) 62
3.4.2.1 Manually creating .bib file 63
3.4.2.2 Creating .bib files using JabRef 67

3.5 Indexes in LaTeX 69

4 Typesetting in LaTeX **73**
4.1 letter class in LaTeX 73
4.2 article class in LaTeX 76
4.3 report class in LaTeX 80
4.4 book class in LaTeX 88

5 Links for LaTeX **91**

Bibliography **93**

Index **95**

List of Tables

1.1 LaTeX compiler commands to use at command line . . . 7
1.2 Alternatives to TeXMaker 8

2.1 Explanation of hello.tex 16
2.2 Common Files in LaTeX 17
2.3 LaTeX packages to typeset article/report/book 19

3.1 LaTeX Text/Fonts style accessing commands with usage . 26
3.2 LaTeX Text/Fonts size manipulation commands 27
3.3 Examples of applying accents to letter 'o' 28
3.4 Some text-mode special characters in LaTeX 28
3.5 Some text-mode special symbols in LaTeX 29
3.6 Mathematical commands for writing mathematical equations 34
3.7 Constructs of tabular environment 39
3.8 Sample table 42
3.9 Constructs of floating environments like table, figure etc... 43

5.1 Links for LaTeX 91

List of Figures

1.1 Starting GUI of TEXMaker 8

2.1 Two living legends of TEX-LATEX-LATEX 2ε- LATEX3 project... 12
2.2 Output of hello.tex 15

3.1 Output showing space handling in LATEX 28
3.2 Output of given code snippet for labelling and referencing 30
3.3 view of Dia IDE 45
3.4 Graphic displayed using figure environment 49
3.5 Wrapped figure 50
3.6 Usage of Subfloat : Some beautiful Birds 52
3.7 The output using thebibliography 61
3.8 JabRef : A java based easy to use free utility for bibliographic management 67
3.9 An output of a sample file for using .bib 70
3.10 Snap of output: the last page containing generated index for the given sample code 71

4.1 Output of letter-template 75
4.2 Output of article-template with some added text 77
4.3 Output of prjttl.tex 87

1 Installation

Objective of this chapter is to give you introduction of LaTeX with its installation procedure. You will learn in this chapter :

(i) what is LaTeX ?

(ii) What are the essential and supportive softwares ?

(iii) How to install essential and supportive softwares ?

(iv) Configuration of MiKTeX .

(v) LaTeX using Command line.

(vi) LaTeX using TeX Maker.

1.1 What is LaTeX ?

LaTeX is a typesetting system for typesetting your documents in beautiful way using WYSIWYM (What You See Is What You Mean.) terminology.Thus here in LaTeX , you gave typesetting instructions to the TeX engine about how to typeset your document just like a markup languages (eg. HTML); and then on behalf of you the TeX engine typesets the document for you. Thus produced documents using LaTeX won't loses its resolution on any system.
The document you are seeing is actually designed in LaTeX .LaTeX is

the first system which differs in **a** and mathematical a and introduced typesetting easier than anything. Symbols like $\sum, \int, \alpha, \beta, \gamma, \mu, \theta, \vartheta, \phi, \varphi, \omega, \Gamma, \Theta, \Phi, \Omega, \times$ were first introduced by LaTeX in a better way in the world of typesetting.LaTeX is a typography system used by scientists, engineers, mathematicians, and researchers for typesetting the scientific documents. LaTeX is also used to design presentations and posters of scientific and general subjects.Almost each and every university worldwide uses LaTeX as her default typesetting system for dissertation, theses, books , and other documentation preparation.

It is better than the regular word processing software as author only need to concentrate on contents rather than formatting details, once a skeletal, the source file, of LaTeX is developed.Unlike usual WYSIWYG (What You See Is What You Get.) way of word processors, LaTeX uses WYSIWYM (What You See Is What You Mean.) terminology to typeset your documents.LaTeX produces the output in the form of .dvi, .ps, or .pdf format.

1.2 Essential and supportive softwares

Follows the description of essential and necessary softwares required for LaTeX . First most essential is the TeX or LaTeX engine. This section talks about all the **LaTeX tools and essentials for windows**. The windows-xp with service pack 3 is the good OS to start with. Follows the list of softwares; irrespective of operating system; to be installed for proper working of LaTeX in sequence as given below.

(i) gs902w32 Ghostscript for postscript definitions and as intermediary library help to TeX engine to convert document in to pdf. You can freely download it from `www.ghostscript.com/`

(ii) gsv49w32 GhostViewer to view PostScript (.ps) files generated using LaTeX. Download Link is `www.ghostscript.com/`

(iii) basic-miktex-2.9.4231 MiKTeX TeX engine for windows . You need to download basic installer first and then update the require modules (in LaTeX terminology packages) from the net. Download link for MiKTeX is `miktex.org/`

(iv) 

TEXMaker is the cross platform TEX Editor . Download link www.xm1math.net/texmaker/

(v) 

Dia, a free vector diagraming tool, can be used to draw the figures to embed in LATEX documents. Download link is dia-installer.de/.

(vi) 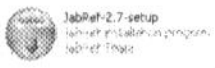

jabref is a java based bibliographic management software. very handy in creating and managing bibliographic databases in LATEX http://jabref.sourceforge.net/

(vii) A pdf reader to read your documents in to pdf form.

(viii) A pdf printer to convert your word and other documents in to pdf form.

1.2.1 How to install the softwares ?

Install the above given softwares in the given sequence. The PDF printer and Dia are not necessary and won't create any problem even if not installed. Rest of the softwares are must and necessary. To Install them all you need to execute the installer and follow the instructions. In the above listed softwares only MiKTEX is for windows, rest are cross platform softwares. Installation process of LATEX is very easy to follow. As LATEX outputs are generally in either postscript(.ps) or portable document format(.pdf); one need to install a postscript first. Here we are using the popular postscript definition package Ghostscript, which is a FOSS(Free open source software) just like LATEX .

1.2.2 Installing Ghostscript

Download the recent version of Ghostscript for your operating system from its site. Double click the installer file, and follow the instruction by pressing Next button on installation dialogue menu. It will be better if you install it first of all other softwares in the above list.

1.2.3 Installing GhostView

If you like to view your output files in postscript formats then this is the must Software to install; procedure is same as above. Only thing that you keep in mind that do not associate it with the .pdf files, as we are having many efficient PDF-reader softwares out there. Also, this software on its every run will ask you about registering it. It's upto you, whether to register or not; but it will be better if you register Ghostview as it help it's developers to keep it running. It won't create any problem even without registration.

1.2.4 Installing MikTEX .

Double click on the basic installer of MiKTEX ,and follow the instructions on installation menu. MiKTEX is FOSS, and authors of this book really appreciate if you donate a small amount to this project as well as any other FOSS tools that you use. Your small donation to FOSS keeps it Free and Open source and readily at your service. After installing MikTEX you need to configure it for the proper use.

1.2.4.1 Configuration of MiKTEX .

After installation of MiKTEX go to "MiKTEX 2.09 directory" and choose "Settings (admin)" from "Maintenance(admin)" and then choose packages tab from it. Select all unselected packages and click on "start package manager". This will install all basic packages and configure automatically your update manager to nearest TEX archive for updation of rest of the packages

After the installation of any package always press the "refresh FNDB" and then "update FORMAT" buttons on "General" TAB of "Settings(Admin)". This will help TEX or LATEX engine to work properly by generating necessary mappings and alteration in settings to develop proper pdf or postscript or dvi documents. Now select "package manager(admin)" from "Maintenance(admin)" and choose desired packages to install and press + sign in upper left corner. This will install all selected packages. You can change package source to "from directory" instead of "from net" by selecting and modifying Repository option in package manager.

For installing packages from disk download the packages from repository and stored it in some directory. Specify the path to this directory, and you can install packages from disk.

After completion of package installation, click "Refresh FNDB" and then "Update format" buttons from Settings (admin). it is always safe to install all the packages on the fly; that means before starting typesetting your first LaTeX document.

1.3 LaTeX using command line

After installation and of the MiKTeX to check whether it is installed properly or not go to command prompt of windows. Create a directory/folder where you want to store all of your LaTeX files, say "latex-practice". And type latex on command prompt. We are having this folder at D: drive. The command sequence is as given below .

```
D:\latex-practice>latex
This is pdfTeX , Version3.1415296-1.40.11 <MiKTeX >
```

If you see the above message , installation is OK. the version of MiKTeX may change as we are expecting you to download and install the recent version of it. if you get above message , that means you are ready to work with LaTeX .
To compile your .tex files , now you only need to type the name of file after command latex or pdflatex without any extension as shown below.

```
D:\latex-practice>pdflatex yourfile
```

If file have no errors then LaTeX will generate the pdf file from your yourfile.tex, or it will show you the errors. We will see the types of errors that can happen using basic LaTeX in second chapter. If you used latex command then you need to usedvi2ps and ps2pdf or dvipdf commands to generate either postscript file or pdf file as latex yourfile generates only .dvi file as final output.
The sequence to generate .ps, the postscript file is

```
D:\latex-practice>latex yourfile
D:\latex-practice>dvi2ps yourfile
```

To genearte .pdf file there are two sequence as given below.

```
D:\latex-practice>latex yourfile
D:\latex-practice>dvi2ps yourfile
D:\latex-practice>ps2pdf yourfile
```

Or , the following

```
D:\latex-practice>latex yourfile
D:\latex-practice>dvipdf yourfile
```

In case you are having bibliography, or glossary or index files included in your LaTeX document, then after `latex` or `pdflatex` command use `bibtex` and `makeindex` command just like above. And, after that use `latex` or `pdflatex` twice.
The usual sequence of compilation of `yourfile.tex` containing commands to generate index, glossary and bibliograpy is as given beneath.
Sequence using `latex` command as initial command

```
D:\latex-practice>latex yourfile
D:\latex-practice>makeindex yourfile
D:\latex-practice>bibtex yourfile
D:\latex-practice>latex yourfile
D:\latex-practice>latex yourfile
D:\latex-practice>dvipdf yourfile
```

And, sequence using `pdflatex` command

```
D:\latex-practice>pdflatex yourfile
D:\latex-practice>makeindex yourfile
D:\latex-practice>bibtex yourfile
D:\latex-practice>pdflatex yourfile
D:\latex-practice>pdflatex yourfile
```

Table 1.1 shows the generally required compilation commands with their explanation. There are many other LaTeX commands which you may need when working with advance LaTeX , which is just out of scope of this book. though the once compiling with `latex / pdflatex` generates the desired output, for proper outcome always compile your LaTeX files twice.

1.4 LaTeX using TeXMaker

TeXMaker is a LaTeX editor. It is easiest editor. It's FOSS(free open source software). There exist many alternatives to TeXMaker. We are giving here either FOSS or freewares only. We found TeXMaker more easy to use than other. You can also try the following FOSS LaTeX editors in table 1.2 which can work on windows. For detail information about them

Table 1.1: LATEX compiler commands to use at command line

Command	Description
`tex`	generates DVI from LaTeX source
`latex`	generates DVI from LaTeX source (the most used one)
`pdftex`	generates PDF from LaTeX source (the most used one)
`pdflatex`	generates PDF from LaTeX source (the most used one)
`dvi2ps`	Converts DVI to postscript
`ps2pdf`	generates PDF from postscript files
`dvipdf`	Converts DVI to PDF
`makeindex`	geneartes intermediate .idx (index description) for creating index in final output. Requires recompilation of the LATEX source for twice using `latex` or `pdflatex` after its application.
`bibtex`	geneartes intermediate .bbl (bibliography descriptions) for creating bibliography in final output. Requires recompilation of the LATEX source for twice using `latex` or `pdflatex` after its application.

visit the respective site. Listed here are few editors among many with which authors of this book practically worked. This book contains information about only those things with which we practically worked. Let's see how to use TEXMaker to create TEX / LATEX documents. Following information only shows how to compile LATEX files using TEXMaker. For complete information about it please refer its website and user manual. When you start a TEXmaker, you will see a GUI(Graphical user interface) as in figure 1.1. The steps to create and compile your LATEX file are as given:

Step 1 Select **New** from **File** menu or from **Icon New** at upper right side below File.

Step 2 Typeset your LATEX document and save it as yourfile.tex

Step 3 Select the compiler from popdown menu(refer figure 1.1 for rest of the steps)

Step 4 Click the arrow before compiler name

Step 5 If TEXMaker shows exited normally message, then select the output type from the popdown menu.

Table 1.2: Alternatives to TEXMaker

Editor	URL and Description
LEd	`www.latexeditor.org/` is a Free feature-rich LATEX editor. One of the good LATEX editor to work with.
Vim	`www.vim.org`Modified VI editor to use for LATEX
TEXniccenter	`www.texniccenter.org` It is just like TEXMaker.
TEXWorks	`http://tug.org/texworks/` Official TEX or LATEX editor. It is by default bundled into the MiKTEX installation.
LyX	`www.lyx.org`It is a quite WYSIWYG LATEX document processor. It is little bit complex to learn but once mastered it's easy. It is one and only freely available WYSIWYG LATEX document processor.

Step 6 Click arrow before View PDF/PS/Dvi to view your output.

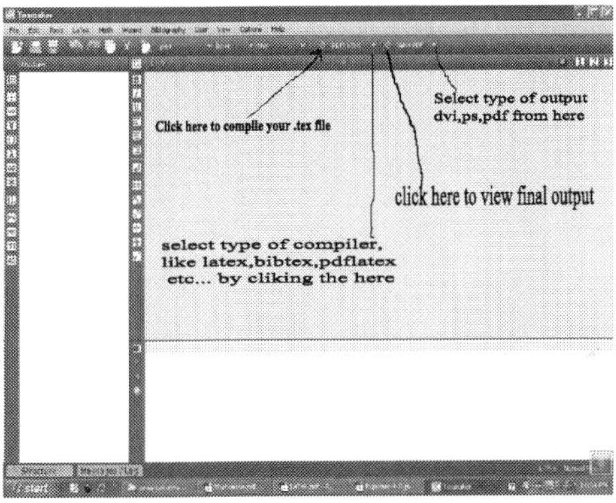

Figure 1.1: Starting GUI of TEXMaker

If LATEX file contains index, bibliography etc. . . then just select compilers from the popdown menu as per the order given in command line usage and compile the LATEX file repeatedly with them. At the end of compilation process just select the proper viewer to see the final output. When you compiles the `.tex` files the TEX-LATEX engine generates many intermediate files to prepare the final output for you. After getting the final

`.pdf` output you may not need these intermediate files; in such case select the `clean option from Tools` menu of TEXMaker, to delete all the intermediate files.

Summary

In this chapter you got all the necessary information about LATEX compiling process and required softwares with the MiKTEX a TEX-LATEX engine for windows with their installation process. You can get more information about TEX-LATEX engines for Linux , Mac , and other operating systems on net. LATEX is purely platform independent; and, so all the information given here is applicable to any platform. There is a cross-platform TEX-LATEX engine called TEXLive available from TEX Users Group `tug.org` which you can get after becoming the member of TUG.TEXMaker and all other editors and softwares are well documented and very easy to use.

2

Enter the LaTeX

Objective of this chapter is to give you introduction of LaTeX typesetting cmputer language. You will learn in this chapter :

(i) History of LaTeX .

(ii) LaTeX versus WYSIWYG word processors .

(iii) The basic LaTeX File structure.

(iv) LaTeX commands and special characters

(v) Errors LaTeX .

(vi) Files in LaTeX .

(vii) LaTeX packages

2.1 History of LaTeX .

History of LaTeX is very interesting story to tell. Prof. Donald Knuth, while writing his book series on art of computer programming faced many problems with available word processors. So he decided to develop a program of typesetting text based on standard editorial practices worldwide. He started writing TeX engine in 1977 , when he faced problems in typesetting his books and articles. with the help of many He released a stable version of TeX in 1982, which get enhanced by the 1989. But TeX just like assembly language, is very tough to master and learn.

In 1990, Leslie Lamport created a macro-package, called LaTeX which

(a) Prof. Donald Knuth (b) Leslie Lamport

Figure 2.1: Two living legends of TeX-LaTeX-LaTeX 2ε- LaTeX3 project...

uses beneath it the TeX engine. LaTeX is pronounced as `Lay-tech` or `Lah-Tech`. LaTeX made TeX easy to use; and today LaTeX 2εbecame a standard typesetting tool for scientific and else writing. Both the living legends, Knuth and Lamport, with many other users and authors of TeX-LaTeX are now preparing for the LaTeX3 project. You will get detail information at `www.latex-project.org` or `www.ctan.org` or `tug.org`.

TeX is extremely stable and platform independent. It is virtually bug free. many authors and user contributed the useful typesetting libraries to it, called packages. Some of which came bundled with most TeX-LaTeX distributions. You can download them from Comprehensive tex archive network `www.ctan.org`.

2.2 LaTeX versus WYSIWYG word processors.

LaTeX is a computer markup language for document processing and hence LaTeX document processing is nothing but the computer programming. here, you creates an input file with extension `.tex`; a simple text file comprising LaTeX commands to typeset your contents. On compilation of this `.tex` file the LaTeX engine turns it in to beautifully typesetted document. This approach used by LaTeX is known as WYSIWYM(What You See Is What you Mean). This has some disadvantages over the WYSIWYG(What You See Is What You Get) approach used by programs such as Openoffice.org writer, Microsoft word and like softwares.

- You can't see the final result straight away when you are typesetting.
- You need to learn the markup language , here in this case it is LATEX.
- It is always not easy to get certain 'looks' for your documents using WYSIWYM.

But, there are certain advantages to the markup language's WYSIWYM approach:

- You can have consistency in layout, tables, fonts, margins etc... throughout the document.
- All sort of scientific and mathematical formulae becomes easy to typeset.
- Adding indices, contents,margin-notes, footnotes, cross referencing, etc... become more easy than WYSIWYG.
- You get a document correctly structured and always in a way you wanted it.

Thus in LATEX you see the logical structure of the document when you LATEXing your document; and LATEX engine takes care of the formatting for you. There are many other advantages which you will learn when you use LATEX consistently atleast for a month. After one month of using LATEX to prepare your documents,the authors of this book are confident enough to claim that you will never ever go to WYSIWYG stuff.

2.3 The basic LATEX File structure.

The basic LATEX file structure for .tex is as given below:

LATEX file structure

```
\documentclass[list of options ]{class type}
%anything after the % sign is considered as comment
%and get ignored.
\usepackage[options list]{packagename}
%you can also add the package names separated with
%comma but we won't promote it
%for including packages in your .tex file.
```

```
%Instead always use separate \usepackage command
%for every package
\renewcommand{new-command-name}{old-command}
% Everything between \documentclass and \begin document
%is called as preamble
%and rarely contain a part of your document
\begin{document}
 Your actual text to typeset goes here
between \begin and \end document.
\end{document}
```

From the above code template you may find LaTeX similar to HTML(Hyper text markup language). It has two parts to define **preamble**, the first part between `\documentclass` and `\begin{ document }`. Preamble contains all the list of packages, LaTeX macros for new commands and environments and definitions globally applied to your document. The second part is **Body** of the LaTeX between `\begin{ document }` and `\end{ document }`, where resides your actual text and rest of the contents like images, tables etc.... Anything written after **%** sign is considered as comment and get ignored by LaTeX . Let's see our first program `hello.tex` and its output in figure2.2 as given below.

`hello.tex`

```
% hello.tex
\documentclass [12pt,a4paper,twocolumn]{article}
\usepackage[pdftex]{graphicx}
\newcommand{\HRule}{\rule{\linewidth}{0.5mm}}
\begin{document}
\HRule \\ Hello world. \\
\HRule \\
\end{document}
```

To obtain the output `hello.pdf` in figure 2.2, you need to compile the `hello.tex` using either `pdftex` or `pdflatex`. Let's see the explanation of the above program(refer table2.1). First line of `.tex` file is always start with the command

`\documentclass[options]{classtype}` ; some of the documentclass types in LaTeX are as given below.

article Used to prepare the scientific research papers, presentations, journals, short reports etc...

Hello world.

Figure 2.2: Output of hello.tex

letter It is used to typeset the letters.

slides As name suggest this is used to create the presentation slides from the research articles.

report This is used to create reports, theses, thesaurus, small books etc...

book Same as `report` but generally used to create a large real books

2.4 LATEX commands and special characters.

As LATEX is a computer language; it has some special characters that you can't directly use to typeset in your document. LATEX acts in two modes, **text mode** and **mathmode**, and in this respect some of the special characters have different commands to typeset them in LATEX .
**# $ % ^ & _ { } ~ ** are the special characters in LATEX and to typeset them except ' \ ' you only need to prefix them with ' \ ' as `\#` , `\$` , `\%` , `\^` `\&` , `\_` , `\{` , `\}` , `\~` . To typeset ' \ ' , in math mode use special command `\backslash`
and in text mode use `\textbackslash` . To typeset space a single ' \ ' with space is used. We will see other commands for typesetting symbols as and when we encounter them.
LATEX commands are case sensitive and always starts with ' \ ' followed by command-name. Command-names consists of letters only and terminates with space, a number or any other non-letter. Options to command are passed through square brackets [ ] and parameters are passed through the braces { }. The general syntax of LATEX command is

```
\commandname[option1,option2,...]{argument1,argument2,...}
```

Table 2.1: Explanation of hello.tex

Program line	**Explanation**
`% hello.tex`	Name of the program. anything after "% " is considered as comment
`\documentclass [12pt,a4paper ,twocolumn]{article}`	The first line of the `hello.tex` declaring the type of document using `\documentclass{ }`;here it is `article`. Options in square brackets are: `12pt`-size of regular text ,`a4paper`-paper-size for document typesetting , and `twocolumn`-number of columns in the document.
`\usepackage [pdftex]{graphicx}`	The `\usepackage` is a command in LATEX to include the standard libraries to handle and introduce some advanced features of LATEX . The `graphicx` package deals with including graphics in LATEX with option of compilation `pdftex` only.
`\newcommand{\HRule} {\rule {\linewidth}{0.5mm}}`	`\newcommand` is the command in LATEX to redefine existing command as per the user's need. Here we redefined `\rule{\linewidth}{.5mm}` as `\HRule` as horizontal rule. The `\linewidth` defines the thickness of line drawn, in this case it is 0.5mm.
`\begin{document}`	Actual contents are entered after the `\begin{document}` environment in LATEX . All the information that you want to typeset must be entered between `\begin{document}` and `\end{document}`
`\end{document}`	This is the last line of LATEX code of typesetting. Anything written after it just get ignored by TEX-LATEX engine.

2.5 Errors in LaTeX .

Perhaps the most feared factor in learning any new skill is what to do when error(s) occurs. don't panic. LaTeX is typesetting language and case sensitive, and 90% of errors in LaTeX are either of misspells of commands or just forgetting the braces.
Error messages begin with an exclamation mark(!)at the start of the line, and give a description of the error, followed by another line starting with the number, which refers to the line-number in your document file which LaTeX was processing when the error was spotted. In TeXMaker, you will see errors and warnings in message/log panel.
Warnings are just the comments by LaTeX for directing you to look in to your LaTeX code for more neatness; and hence warnings can be overlooked.

2.6 Files in LaTeX .

Apart from the main input file; **.tex** LaTeX have many other files, most of which are intermediaries. Follows the descriptions of some most common files, table2.2, that you might encounter while LaTeXing. Though you need to clear out all intermediary files after getting final output in pdf format; knowing these files will really help you to understand the internal working of LaTeX. This will obviously help those who want to use LaTeX for typesetting all their documents.

Table 2.2: Common Files in LaTeX

File type	**Description**
.tex	Main input file for containing typesetting information.
.sty	Style or package files, which get loaded in to the `.tex` file using `\usepackage[options]{packagename}` command.
.cls	Class file defining class type like article , report, slides etc...
.dtx	Documented TeX. It is the main distribution format for `.sty` files.
.ins	Installer file for `.dtx`. On LaTeXing `.ins` file you will get `.dtx` file.
.fd	Font description file.

Table 2.2: (continued)

File type	Description
.toc	File containing the information about section headers and used to create `tableofcontents` on further compilation of `.tex` file.
.lof	File containing the information about figure headers and used to create `listoffigures` on further compilation of `.tex` file.
.lot	File containing the information about table headers and used to create `listoftables` on further compilation of `.tex` file.
.log	a Log file giving every detail information about the compilation process; i.e. all errors, warnings .
.idx	LATEX stores all the words that go into the index in this file. Process this file with `makeindex`.
.ind	The processed `.idx`file for creating index in output file.
.ilg	Log file for index file compilation details.
.aux	Auxiliary file for storing information about cross referencing.
.dvi	Primary output file for LATEX stands for device independent.
.ps	Secondary output file of LATEX .
.pdf	Secondary output file of LATEX and Primary output file for PDFLATEX .

2.7 LATEX packages

Packages are the most important ready made function libraries contributed by many developer-users of LATEX to help us in typesetting the intended documents in very beautiful and mesmerizing ways.There are around 2000+ registered packages available for MiKTEX , a LATEX distribution for Windows. And, plenty more available from many users which won't come with default MiKTEX distribution. Even you can define your own packages as per your need and requirements. How to create your own package is just kept out of the scope of this book, just to make it more precise and handy.

In this book, as required by the scope of the book, We are focusing on those registered packages, table2.3, which are necessary and sufficient to typeset your small book or theses or project report or dissertation.

Usage command for packages is `\usepackage[options]{packagename}` .

You also can use packages in one command just by separating package names using commas, but we prefer and recommend not to do this.

Table 2.3: LaTeX packages to typeset article/report/book

Package Name	**Description about Usage**
mathptmx **amsmath** **amsfonts** **amssymb**	Required for mathematical typesetting. such as Mathematical equations. mathematical fonts typesetting. mathematical symbols typesetting.

hyperref	Used for hyperlinking/cross-referencing of document's parts or sections which each other. it automatically loads `nameref` package. Follows the declaration syntax for it.
	`\usepackage[bookmarks=true, unicode=false,`
	`pdftoolbar=true, pdfmenubar=true,`
	`pdffitwindow=true, %pdftitle={My title},`
	`%pdfauthor={Author}, %pdfsubject={Subject},`
	`%pdfnewwindow=true,`
	`colorlinks=true,`
	`linkcolor=black,`
	`%citecolor=green,`
	`%filecolor=magenta,`
	`%urlcolor=cyan`
	`]{hyperref}`

graphicx	Required to import external graphics in to LaTeX document.After declaring this package you can use the following command to imports external files in your LaTeX document. If you are compiling with LaTeX then you can use **.eps(Encapsulated PostScript)** Format. When you are compiling with PDFLaTeX you can use **.JPG/.JPEG, .PNG , .PDF** formats to include images in your document. To create images you can use any suitable software capable to generate above formats. The syntax of command for importing images is as given `\includegraphics[imgoptions]{./imgpath/imgname}` we will see the detailed usage later in chapter3.

Table 2.3: (LaTeX packages. . . continued.)

Package Name	Description about Usage
subfig	Many time in one head you have more than one images; in such situation you required to use this package. This package provide the following command `\subfloat[subcaption]{ \includegraphics[.]{.}}` to include many images within one head.We will see it in detailed in chapter3.
array	To create arrays or tables of large length you required to declare this package before `longtable` package.
longtable	Provides an `longtable` environment to create a table which is spread over more than one page.We will see it in detailed in chapter3.
multirow	Provides a command to span the row; and the command is `\multirow{number-of-rows}{width}{contents}`
color or **xcolor**	Useful to manipulate text or page color. To design color tables etc. . . We will see its usage in chapter3.

fancyhdr	Useful to create fancy headers and footers with respect to chapters and sections in report/book. The brief usage detail is as given :
	`\usepackage{fancyhdr}`
	`\pagestyle{fancy}`
	`\lhead{}`
	`\chead{}`
	`\rhead{{\tiny \rightmark}}`
	`\lfoot{{\tiny  \leftmark}}`
	`\cfoot{}`
	`\rfoot{\thepage}`
	Rest details we will see in chapter3.

fncychap	Package providing seven predefined chapter heading styles to choose from. the seven styles are :**Sonny , Lenny , Glenn , Conny , Rejne , Bjarne , Bjornstrup** .The usage detail as is given :
	`\usepackage[Bjornstrup`
	`]{fncychap}`

Table 2.3: (LaTeX packages. . . continued.)

Package Name	Description about Usage
paralist	Introduces inline lists environment and list numbering/sequencing manipulation tricks. We will see its usage details in chapter3.
makeidx	Package to make indexes of useful terms at the end of report/book. In preamble you must declared it strictly as given below; any deviation to this will cause an error. `\usepackage{makeidx}` `\makeindex` In the body of your main `.tex` file you must then add command `\printindex` We will see its usage details in chapter3.
geometry	This package is very useful to define page margins. We won't refer to change default margins setted up by LaTeX ; but incase you required to do so use the following declaration in your preamble. `\usepackage[top=tlength, bottom=blength,left=llength, right=rlength]{geometry}` Where length can be defined in pt(points), mm(millimetre), or cm(centimetre). For the other usage of this package refer chapter3.

2.7.1 The Preamble of report/Book

From the above you can get an idea about how the preamble of your report , book, theses, or dissertation will look like. For this book we defined the preamble as given below. You will learn additional commands in it, in next chapters.

PREAMBLE OF REPORT/BOOK

```
\documentclass[12pt,a4paper,twoside,openright]{book}
%\usepackage{geometry}
\usepackage{mathptmx}
\usepackage[bookmarks=true,
unicode=false,
pdftoolbar=true, pdfmenubar=true,
```

```
pdffitwindow=true, %pdftitle={My title},
%pdfauthor={Author},
%pdfsubject={Subject},
%pdfnewwindow=true,
colorlinks=true,
linkcolor=black,
%citecolor=green,
%filecolor=magenta,
%urlcolor=cyan
]{hyperref}
\usepackage{amsmath}
\usepackage[pdftex]{graphicx}
\usepackage{subfig}
\usepackage{array}
\usepackage{longtable}
\usepackage{multirow}
\usepackage{color}
\usepackage[Bjornstrup]{fncychap}
\usepackage{makeidx}
\makeindex
\usepackage{paralist}
\usepackage{fancyhdr}
\pagestyle{fancy}
\lhead{}
\chead{}
\rhead{{\tiny \rightmark}}
\lfoot{{\tiny  \leftmark}}
\cfoot{}
\rfoot{\thepage}
\setcounter{secnumdepth}{4}
\setcounter{tocdepth}{3}
\renewcommand{\headrulewidth}{0.5pt}
\renewcommand{\footrulewidth}{0.5pt}
\newcommand{\HRule}{\rule{\linewidth}{0.5mm}}
\begin{document}
        .
        .
\end{document}
```

Summary

In this chapter you got all the necessary information about: History of LaTeX . A comparison between LaTeX versus WYSIWYG word processors answering why you should use LaTeX over WYSIWYG. Explanation of the basic input file `.tex` structure for LaTeX with possible errors that may occur in LaTeXing, and all the necessary packages required to typeset a better report/book. As LaTeX is purely platform independent; and, so all the information given here is applicable to any platform.

3

LaTeX Commands & Environments

Objective of this chapter is to give you introduction of commands and environments in LaTeX typesetting computer language . You will learn in this chapter :

(i) Text-mode commands in LaTeX .

(ii) Math-mode commands in LaTeX .

(iii) Environments in LaTeX .

(iv) Bibliographies in LaTeX .

(v) Indexes in LaTeX .

To typeset a better document, it is an essential thing to know the typesetting commands and environments that LaTeX offers to you. LaTeX operates in two modes, text & math, and have a set of commands to use in them. LaTeX , also offers environments like table , figure , & listings to typeset tables,import images, and like... This chapter will explained you all such commonly used LaTeX Commands & Environments. The information included is very helpful to typeset a better document using LaTeX .If not mentioned about where to use the commands given then commands explain below are specifically used in the **body** of the LaTeX document; part between the `\begin{document}` & `\end{document}` .

3.1 Text-mode commands in LATEX

Text-mode commands are those which are used to create some text manipulation. We had already seen special characters in chapter2,section2.4. Now we will see the rest of text manipulation commands.

3.1.1 Text style & size manipulation commands

Following commands, table3.1can be used to manipulate the look of text in your document. LATEX by default uses **cmr(computer modern roman)** font as output font for its document.

Table 3.1: LATEX Text/Fonts style accessing commands with usage

LATEX command	output
`\textbf{Your text}`	**Your text**
`\textit{Your text}`	*Your text*
`\textsc{Your text}`	YOUR TEXT
`\textrm{Your text}`	Your text
`\textsf{Your text}`	Your text
`\textsl{Your text}`	*Your text*
`\texttt{your text}`	`Your text`

To manipulate the size of the text, LATEX refers fontsize declared in `option part of documentclass` as base font size. Following table3.2 shows size manipulation commands with there`output with respect to font size 12pt` declared in option of documentclass declaration.
The scale of Font size manipulation for the above commands in pt(points) is
-2 -1 -1 -1 basesize +2 +2 +3 +3 +5 pt. So if **basefontsize is 10 pt** then we get **tiny=5pt, scriptsize=7pt, footnotesize=8pt, small=9pt, normalsize=10pt, large=12pt, Large=14pt, LARGE=17pt , huge=20pt, and Huge=25pt** as the size of diplayed text.

3.1.2 Text handling in LATEX

Apart from the above LATEX has some good features of text handling; which every author find useful to work with. Following example code will illustrate this

Table 3.2: LATEX Text/Fonts size manipulation commands

LATEX Command	Output
`\tiny{Your text}`	Your text
`\scriptsize{Your text}`	Your text
`\footnotesize{Your text}`	Your text
`\small{Your text}`	Your text
`\normalsize{Your text}`	Your text
`\large{Your text}`	Your text
`\Large{your text}`	Your text
`\LARGE{your text}`	Your text
`\huge{your text}`	Your text
`\Huge{your text}`	Your text

EXAMPLE CODE

```
This                         is an example code\\
Where
you
will
find the white space treatment of \LaTeX\ .

A blank line means start of new paragraph




And more than a blank line means same.
If you are writing something that you do not want
 to break  it then
 just use \verb+ \mbox{yourdata} + \\like
\verb+  \mbox{1264  45745 65454} +
and you will get this result.\\
 \mbox{1264  45745 65454}
   else you will get 1264  45745 65454 this result
```

The output of the above code is as given in figure 3.1
The above example shows that LATEX replaces `n number of spaces with single space` . A single or more blank line(s) in text is indica-

This is an example code
Where you will find the white space treatment of LATEX .
A blank line means start of new paragraph
And more than a blank line means same. If you are writing something that you do not want to break it then just use \mbox{yourdata}
like \mbox{1264 45745 65454} and you will get this result.
1264 45745 65454 else you will get 1264 45745 65454 this result

Figure 3.1: Output showing space handling in LATEX

tion of new paragraph. The command `\verb+ command name +` is used to display the LATEX commands. The `\\` means newline. and `\mbox{data}` keeps data together.

3.1.3 Accents & Special Characters/Symbols

LATEX supports the use of accents and special characters from many languages. The table 3.3 shows use of all sort of such accents with letter ‘o’; you can also apply same to other letters.

Table 3.3: Examples of applying accents to letter ‘o’

command	output	command	output	command	output	command	output
\`o	ò	\'o	ó	\~o	õ	\^o	ô
\=o	ō	\.o	ȯ	\"o	ö	\u o	ŏ
\v o	ǒ	\H o	ő	\c o	o̧	\d o	ọ
\o	ø	\b o	o̲	\t o	o͡	\O	Ø

The table 3.4 shows some special characters and table 3.5 shows some symbols using LATEX commands in `text mode`.

Table 3.4: Some text-mode special characters in LATEX

command	output	command	output	command	output	command	output
\oe	œ	\OE	Œ	\ae	æ	\AE	Æ
\aa	å	\AA	Å	\l	ł	\L	Ł
\i	ı	\j	▮	!`	¡	?`	¿

There are many more symbols available in LATEX. We, here only given

Table 3.5: Some text-mode special symbols in LaTeX

command	output	command	output
`\textcopyright`	©	`\textregistered`	®
`\textparagraph`	¶	`\texttrademark`	™
`\ldots`	...	`\textbullet`	•

those which we need most while typesetting our project report. More often the `math-mode` alternatives to the `text-mode` symbols are used by the typesetters.

3.1.4 Selecting Fonts for typesetting

LaTeX by default uses **cmr** computer modern roman type font, which is good enough to have no need to change the output font of the document. But, in case you won't want your document in **cmr**; you can add following command in **preamble** to make changes in output font.

```
\fontencoding{\encodingdefault}
\fontfamily{\familydefault}
\fontseries{\seriesdefault}
\fontshape{\shapedefault}
\selectfont
```

The values of these attribute variables may be changed using `\renewcommand` , for example `\renewcommand{\familydefault}{\sfdefault}` causes the entire document to be set in the default sans serif font. For further details please refer the font installation & selection guide of LaTeX distribution.

3.1.5 Labelling & cross-referencing

Labelling & cross-referencing is very essential. It is used for cross referencing and linking the main terms within a textual content. For its full operation add `\usepackage[...]`
`{hyperref}` in the preamble. The snippet of code for labelling and referencing with its output(refer figure 3.2) is as shown below. To obtain proper output always compile .tex file twice using PDFLaTeX.

SNIPPET OF CODE

```
\subsection{Labelling \& cross-referencing }
Labelling \& cross-referencing is very essential.
It is used for cross referencing and linking the main
terms within a textual content. For its full operation
add \verb+ \usepackage[...]{hyperref} +
in the preamble. The snippet of code for
labelling and referencing with
its output(refer figure \ref{fig:lcr})
is as shown below.
To obtain proper output always compile
.tex file twice using PDFLaTeX.
\begin{figure}[!h]
\centering
\includegraphics[scale=.7]{./ch3/lcr}
\caption{Output of given code snippet for
labelling and referencing\label{fig:lcr}}
\end{figure}
```

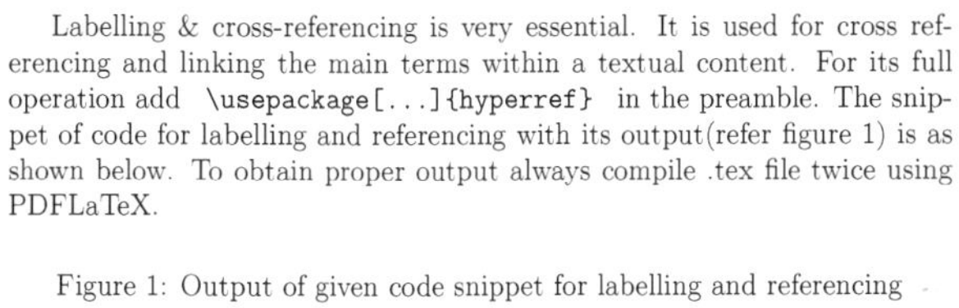
Labelling & cross-referencing is very essential. It is used for cross referencing and linking the main terms within a textual content. For its full operation add `\usepackage[...]{hyperref}` in the preamble. The snippet of code for labelling and referencing with its output(refer figure 1) is as shown below. To obtain proper output always compile .tex file twice using PDFLaTeX.

Figure 1: Output of given code snippet for labelling and referencing

Figure 3.2: Output of given code snippet for labelling and referencing

Labelling and cross referencing allow you to refer any content of your document which is numbered.
`\label{mark}` command can be used for labelling chapters, sections, lists, etc... while `\ref{mark}` is used to refer the marked content by its number. If you want to refer the particular page use `\pageref{mark}` instead of `\ref{mark}` command. If there exist no `\label{mark}` for `\ref{mark}` or `\pageref{mark}` then LaTeX will replace `\ref{mark}` or `\pageref{mark}` with "??".

3.1.6 chapter, section and part

The commands `\part*{part name}`, `\part{part name}`, `\chapter*{chapter name}` and `\chapter{chapter name}` are allowed only in report/book class or other advanced classes in LaTeX which are useful in creating either a report or book. The starred (" * ") version of the commands generates the part/chapter names with no numbers, while **plain** version of these commands Auto-number the part/chapter in increasing order with respective command appearance in the **.tex** file.
In same fashion LaTeX provides `\section*{section name}`, `\section{section name}` commands; which can be used in all classes except **letter** to create non-numbered or numbered section names.
Similarly, `\subsection*{subsection name}` , `\subsection{subsection name}` commands creates subsection names; and
`\subsubsection*{subsubsection name}` , `\subsubsection{subsubsection name}` commands creates non-numbered and auto-numbered subsubsection names.

3.1.6.1 Styling chapter names

By default part is aligned at center of page, while chapter name and section names are aligned to left. Incase one won't like default style of chapter naming, then use package **fncychap** with one of its chapter title style as given in table 2.3 in chapter 2 for chapter name style and alignment.

3.1.7 Boxed text

Boxes can be used to show the significance of text or mathematical formulae. It is very good typesetting way to make your text/points/math stand out from the regular text. A simple `\mbox{98    90    45}` command will produce the result 98 90 45 which is boxed text without any box frame. A simple `\fbox{98    90    45}` command will produce the result $\boxed{\text{98 90 45}}$ which is boxed text with box frame. But if the text within box exceeds the line length then we will get following undesirable results using above said commands.

```
\mbox{which is boxed text
with box frame.
But if the text within box exceeds the line
```